HOMEOWNER'S GUIDE TO
Training & Pruning Apple Trees

~

Secrets to Success, from Planting to Maturity

STEVE W. CHADDE

"Anyone who has a garden, park or orchard tree has an opportunity to ensure that it offers protection, brings beauty and bears fruit for future generations. In short, every one of us should aspire to be a forester." — GABRIEL HEMERY

Homeowner's Guide to Training and Pruning Apple Trees
Steve W. Chadde

Copyright © 2020 by Steve W. Chadde
All rights reserved.
Published in the United States of America

ISBN: 9781951682200

The author can be reached at *steve@orchardinnovations.com*

Contents

Introduction 5
Getting Started... 7
The Growing Parts 8
Application 10
Growing to the Sun 11
The Three Types of Pruning Cuts 12
Timing 12
Here are the Answers 15
FROM PLANTING TO MATURITY...STEP-BY-STEP 18
    Spring of Year One 18
    Cultivate, Fertilize, Mulch 18
    Summer of Year One 20
    Spring of Year Two 22
    Star Growth 22
    Summer of Year Two 23
    Bending the Twig 24
    The Christmas Tree 26
    Years Three and Four 27
    Limit its Height 28
    Forever After... 28
Pruning a Neglected Fruit Tree 29
Other Fruit Trees 31
    Pear 31
    Sweet Cherry 31
    Sour Cherry and European Plum 32
    Peach and Japanese Plums 33
    Apricot 34
    Persimmon 34
    Fig 34
Basic Terms 35
Appendix. Tree Training Supplies 36

As you'll learn how in this guide, proper training and pruning applied each year will develop your apple tree into the ideal conical, "Christmas-tree" shape (see page 26). Limb spreaders are an invaluable tool to help accomplish this goal.

Introduction

In contrast to modern commercial orchards consisting of closely planted trees attached to a trellis, backyard growers will find it easiest to train apple trees to a central leader with several tiers of lateral (or scaffold) branches. This guide will teach you, step-by-step, how to train your young fruit tree (with a focus on apple trees), from planting to maturity, developing the ideal "Christmas tree" shape. Along the way, we'll reveal our "insider's secrets" to help you understand the 'whys' of tree growth and how each type of pruning cut affects your tree. Finally, once your tree reaches the desired height, we'll share with you a simple method to keep your tree within bounds.

Why train apple trees?

- Training develops a strong tree that can support heavy crop-loads without breaking its limbs.
- Training brings a young tree into production earlier than an untrained tree.
- Training develops a more open, healthier tree, and apples with better color

Why prune apples trees?

- Pruning reduces overall tree size.
- Pruning makes trees easier to spray and harvest.
- Pruning young trees improves their strength and helps induce branching.
- Pruning trees increases the amount and quality of their fruit.
- Pruning reduces the need to prop up fruit-laden branches.

General rules for training your apple tree

- Use dwarfing rootstocks for easier training and earlier harvests.
- Begin training at planting and continue for the life of the tree.
- Remove unwanted shoots in summer when they're small.
- Train more by limb positioning than by pruning.

General rules for pruning

- Prune trees at planting time to balance the tops with the roots.
- Prune young trees very lightly – heavy pruning will delay fruiting.
- Prune mature trees more heavily, especially if growth has been little.
- Prune the top branches of the tree more heavily than the lower branches.
- Prune when all danger from fall or early winter freeze has passed, but before full bloom in spring.
- In a mature tree, thin out more of the shoots that grow toward the end of a well-pruned branch. This increases fruit size and quality on the remaining shoots

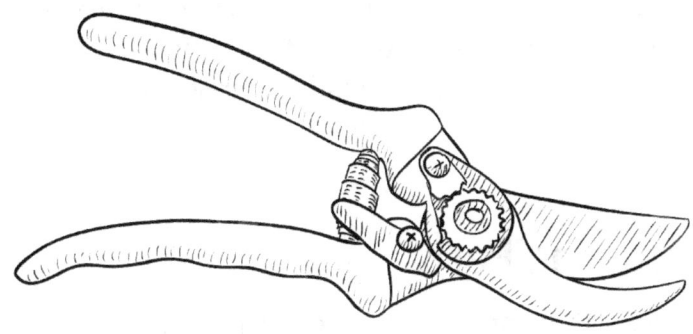

Getting Started...

Tired of pruning those apple trees as if you were blindfolded? Do you worry about doing it all wrong? Maybe you don't prune at all or very little because of the fear of making a mistake. Do situations like the following puzzle you?

1. You plant a new tree; it is five feet tall but has no side branches. You want to have the first branches form at about 20" from the ground. What do you do?

2. You plant a new tree that is only 3 feet tall. A tree this size is weak. It needs to be stimulated to grow. How would you prune it in order to accomplish this?

3. You have a two-year old tree; one limb is very long and the rest are much shorter. How do you correct this?

4. You planted a tree this spring; now it is July and the tree hasn't produced nice, long, new shoots like it was supposed to. What should you do?

5. Your older apple tree is too big and thick with vigorous limbs and shoots. Where do you begin to correct it?

6. Your older apple tree is much too tall. How can you make it shorter without making a mess of the tree?

Let's start by giving the background you'll need to make intelligent decisions in pruning and training your apple trees. We're going to let you in on the secrets of how the tree grows and responds to your handling. Once you understand this, training and pruning will be a breeze.

The Growing Parts

The living portion of the tree is called meristematic tissue. This is located at the tips of the shoots, branches, and spurs as a **meristematic cap**, and just inside the bark as a single cell tissue called the **cambium**.

Meristematic cap

Let's focus on the cap first. The meristematic cells in the apex (tip) of the shoot divide forming other cells below and beside themselves.

These new cells enlarge and then become fixed in size. During the growing season new cells continue further to be formed and enlarge; it is because of this continual process that the shoots become longer. The area of elongation is confined to a short area of the tip. Picture the building of a multi-scoop ice cream cone – once a scoop is in place it does not get any larger, but the cone, as a whole, can by adding more scoops.

The **cambium** is a continuous single-layer cylinder of cells which surrounds the shoot. It divides, forming cells in the shape of elongated tubes. The cells formed on the inside of the cylinder are called the **xylem** and carry water and nutrients from the root to the rest of the tree. The cells formed on the outside of the cylinder are called the **phloem** and transport the food manufactured by the leaves throughout the top of the tree and down to the roots. As division continues, the older tubes (xylem and phloem) become plugged and then crushed, ceasing to function as part of the transport system.

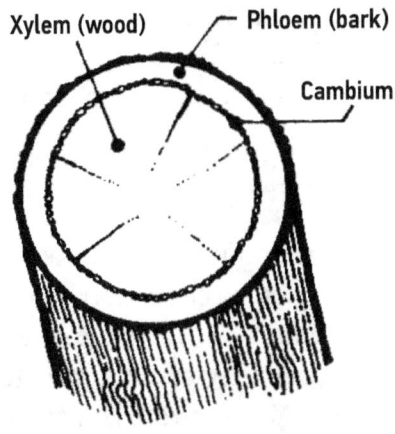

These old xylem cells are the woody portion of the tree, and the old phloem cells, the bark. The continual division of the cambium results in an increase in the circumference of the shoot.

Well, what does it all mean?

First of all, because there is no elongation of any part of the tree except at the growing points, a limb which forms and grows in the tree will always be in the same place as first formed. If this is one foot from the ground, it will always be one foot from the ground until you cut it off. Also limbs will not move further from or closer to one another. The body of the tree is very stable and you can depend on it

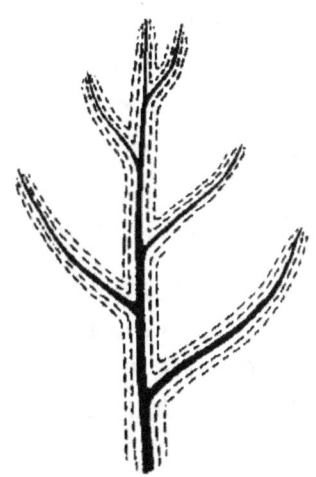

The limbs appear closer because they are fatter (increased in diameter)

remaining that way. It is true that the limbs will appear to grow closer to one another as they get fatter because of the cambial activity, and you may even have to stoop a little to mow under some limbs but the limb has just grown, not moved.

Application

What lessons should we learn from all this information?

1. When pruning, choose limbs that are high enough from the ground. They will not get any higher.

2. Leave enough room between the *framework limbs* to allow for the increase in circumference. "Framework limbs" just refers to the **permanent limbs you are going to choose to form your tree** (these are often also referred to as **"scaffold" limbs**. We'll discuss this in detail later on. How much room is enough? Usually no less than 12".

3. When a branch grows forming a very narrow angle with the trunk, and as both the branch and the trunk continue to grow, the bark (dead phloem tissue) of the limb pushes against the bark of the trunk. Bark, being **non-meristematic,** cannot grow together (unite) so a very weak union is formed. When a heavy crop comes (or the kids climb on the limb), it may split off, ruining the shape of the tree. *Selecting nice wide angles will avoid this "bark inclusion" and the resulting weakness.*

4. If you destroy a section of the cambium, i.e., run into it with the mower, or put a clothesline around the trunk for a long period of time, or forget to take the tag and strings off of a newly planted tree, the tree will be *girdled,* and the transport of water from the roots to the top and food from the top to the root will be stopped, causing the tree to die.

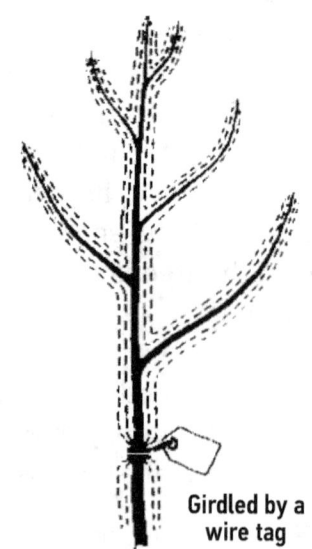

Girdled by a wire tag

Growing to the Sun

Now let's shift direction to understand how the tree grows. Limbs grow toward the sun; that this is because the sun slightly injures the cells on the top of the branch causing them to grow more slowly than those on the bottom of the limb which are not damaged. This uneven growth pushes the tip of the limb upward.

This upright growth habit is normal. but be aware, **upright growing limbs** are more vigorous (they grow faster) than limbs which are kept more horizontal. and upright vigorous limbs are generally vegetative (**not very fruitful**). On the other hand, the more **horizontal limbs** are less vegetative and **more fruitful**. This is all due to how rapidly the **carbohydrates** (food manufactured in the leaves) flow out of the limb, plus some rearrangement of the growth hormones in the limb which change shoot buds to fruiting buds. The steeper the angle of the limb, the faster the carbohydrates will flow out of the limb. We will be talking about the significance of this later, so for now, read on.

Upright vigorous limbs: less fruitful

Horizontal limbs: more fruitful

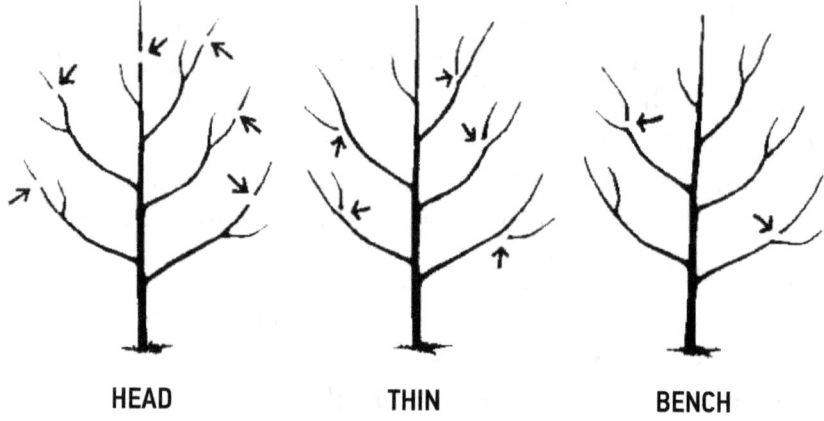

HEAD   THIN   BENCH

The Three Types of Pruning Cuts

What happens when we take out our trusty pruning shears and start to cut this tree? The first thing you need to know is that there are two types of cuts. possibly three. A **heading cut,** where only a portion of the shoot or branch is removed; a **thinning cut,** where the entire limb, shoot, or branch is removed; and a **bench cut,** where a portion of the limb or branch is removed to a point where a side branch has developed. It is important to understand the differences.

Timing

There are two times during the year you may prune your apple tree – **winter and summer.** Actually the first is the period from dormancy (winter and spring before any growth) until the tree blossoms, and the second is in July and August. The tree responds differently to pruning in the dormant season than it does in the summer. A **heading cut** in the dormant to bloom period **stimulates** the rest of the branch. It causes the side buds to grow from the cut down about 16 inches. Why? Because when you make this cut you remove the **dominant terminal bud.** The buds closest to the cut will grow the most and form narrow angles; the buds further down will grow more slowly with wider angles. **The width of the angle is determined by the presence of a growth hormone.** This hormone is manufactured in the growing shoots and then trans-located down the branch. It lodges above the new shoot buds and prevents narrow angles from forming.

The top three shoots grow first. The hormone they produce is then trans-located down the stem to the lower shoots. The top shoots are narrow-angled because they grow before any hormone is present. The other branches below them receive enough hormone from the top shoots to be wide-angled.

Not only does a heading cut in the dormant season cause the limb to grow more vigorously and produce more side shoots, but it also makes it less flexible. This is important if you are planning on the limb spreading under the weight of the fruit or if you plan to physically pull the limb into a more horizontal position sometime in the future. You should also know that the more upright and vigorous the limb on which you make a heading cut, the more rapidly it will grow.

The same heading cut made in the summer will not stimulate much regrowth. Instead it will cause some of the buds to change from vegetative buds into fruit buds for the next season. Pruning in July and August **slows the growth** of the limb being pruned, **does not** force side shoot growth, and **does not** cause the remaining portion of the limb to stiffen.

Thinning cuts do not stimulate much growth whether done in the winter or summer. Be careful with this one; you might think you are making a thinning cut but leave a short stub of a limb. If this is done it will react as if you had made a heading cut. So make sure you cut them completely out. Even though little growth stimulation is expected from a thinning cut, removing a large limb will result in a profusion of **suckers** close to the cut. What is a sucker? It's a new shoot which grows vigorously in a part of the tree where it is not needed. Suckers are like weeds. Weeds are defined as "a plant out of place."

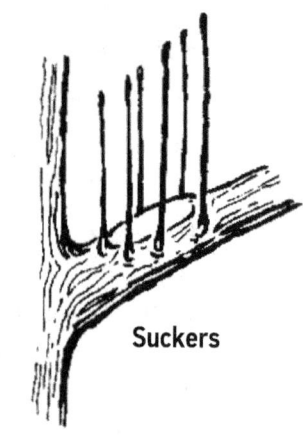
Suckers

RIGHT   WRONG
Don't leave stubs when making thinning cuts

A **bench cut** will stiffen the branch any time it is made (winter or summer).

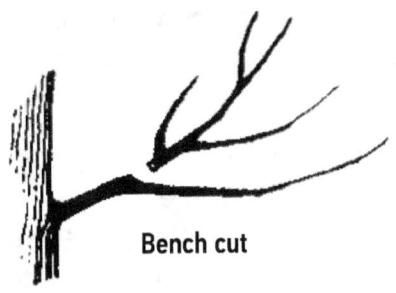
Bench cut

Now, how does all of this fit into pruning? You are about to learn the secrets to successfully pruning and training your tree. With this information, you'll be able to change the system for any special conditions you may encounter.

Here are the Answers

Let's apply the information we've learned so far to the pruning problems presented at the beginning of our discussion.

1. You plant a new tree; it is five feet tall but has no side branches. You want to have the first branches form at about 20" from the ground. What do you do?

First, you make a heading cut no higher than 36" from the ground while the tree is dormant. This cut will initiate growth down about 16" from the point of cut and so you should get good wide-angled side branches in the area 20" above the ground and on up the tree. A heading cut at 32" will guarantee growth at 20". Remember the upper three shoots will be narrow-angled, the lower branches will be wide angled, and the whole tree will be stimulated to grow.

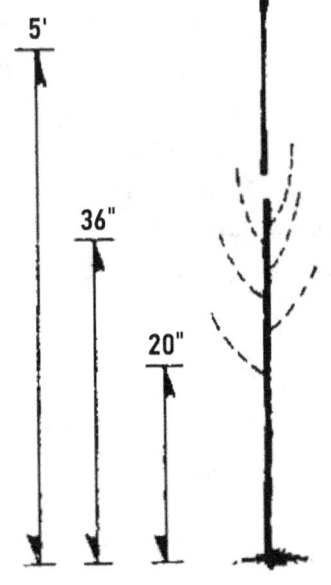

2. You plant a new tree that is only 3 feet tall. A tree this size is weak. It needs to be stimulated to grow. How would you prune it in order to accomplish this?

Start by making a heading cut to about 20" from the ground. This will force the extra growth you need, especially from the top buds, giving you new wood on which to start forming good "framework" branches the *next year*. This cut will also force side branches to form closer to the ground than you desire. You can rub them off with your hand when they are 2 inches long or less. If they grow longer, remove them with a thinning cut.

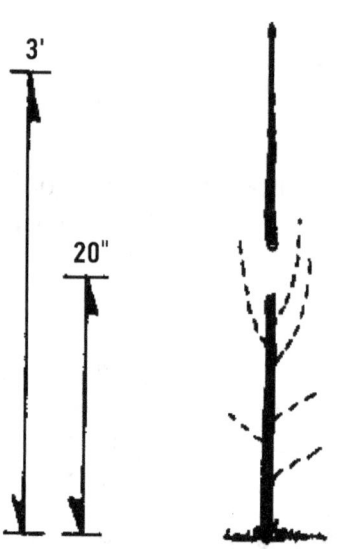

3. You have a two year old tree; one limb is very long and the rest are much shorter. How do you correct this?

If you cut the long one in the spring, it will only grow more strongly, so it is best to pull the long limb into a more horizontal position in order to slow its growth. *Do not head it back!* Make early spring heading cuts on the other limbs to force them to grow more rapidly. In the *summer* you may head back the longer limb to balance with the others.

4. You planted a tree this spring; now it is July and the tree hasn't produced nice long new shoots like it was supposed to. What should you do?

Above all, *do not make heading cuts in the summer;* this will only slow down growth. It is best to cultivate a 3 foot area around the tree, fertilize, mulch, and when needed, water the tree to see if you can stimulate more growth. Next spring make as many heading cuts on side branches as possible and be sure to head the leader back far enough to force growth. Cut away at least 25% of the height of the tree.

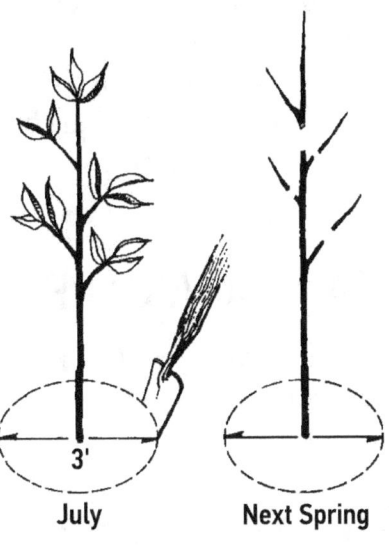

July   Next Spring

5. Your older apple tree is too big and thick with vigorous limbs and shoots. Where do you begin to correct it?

First, you must confine all of your pruning to the **summer pruning** time period (July and August) for the next **two years**. Cut back those limbs that are too long by cutting back to the point where there are apples. Next, **remove** (thinning cuts only) all top and inside suckers. Following this method will not stimulate excessive growth in the tree and will allow you to control the tree.

> "A heading cut in the dormant season causes the limbs to grow more vigorously."

6. Your older apple tree is much too tall. How can you make it shorter without making a mess of the tree?

In the **SPRING,** remove the limbs or portions of limbs necessary to reduce the height of the tree to an acceptable place. This will then cause a lot of new growth to develop at the cut points ... so in August remove (thinning cuts only) all of the upright suckers in the top and throughout the tree. **Head back** all of the other branches to the point where there are apples ... this will help to slow down the excess growth and allow you to control the height of the tree. If there are no apples, head back to a downward growing limb or a bud on the underside of the branch. The limb should end up being shorter than those below.

TRAINING AND PRUNING TIME

Now let's start to train a young apple tree and follow it through to maturity.

Spring of Year One

Most of the trees you buy will have some side branches. These branches may or may not be at the right place once you have planted the tree. So ... to determine this you must first plant the tree. Now that was easy wasn't it? Do you have a good wide-angled branch somewhere between 15 and 20 inches above the 30" ground? If so, make a heading cut so as to remove about 25% of its length. Now let's look for other side branches we might be able to keep. Oh yes, those nice branches that are too close to the ground have to be cut off. Use a thinning cut and cut as close to the stem of the tree as possible. You say they are all less than 15 inches above the ground? Then

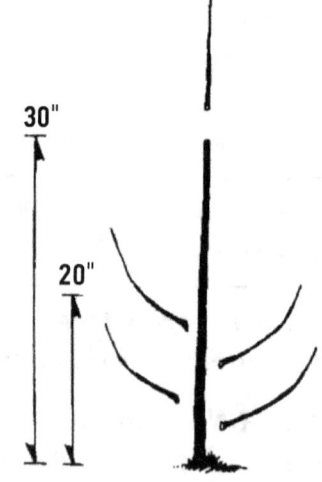

remove **all** of them and make a heading cut on the stem (we will call the stem the **leader** from now on) about 30 inches from the ground.

Let's go back to those of you who are fortunate enough to have usable branches on your new apple tree. Your aim is to choose branches that **balance** the tree. An apple tree's branches grow from the "leader" (remember, this is our new word for the center stem) in a star fashion.

Try to pick those that best balance the tree, maybe

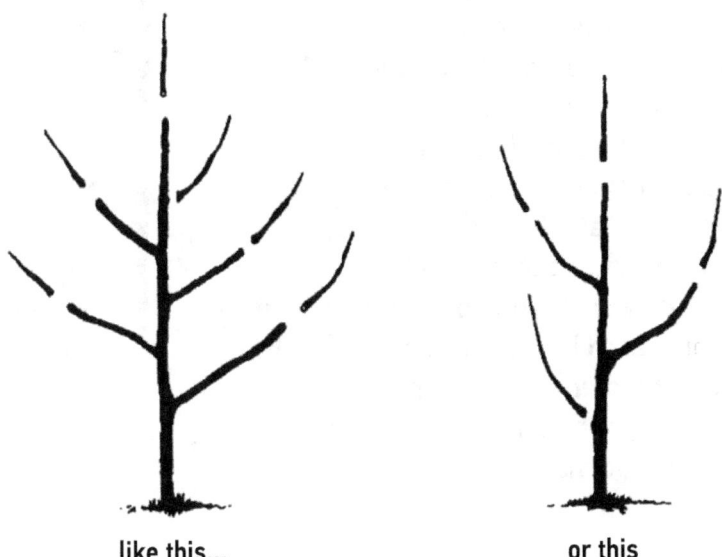

like this...   or this

Make a heading cut on the branches you kept, removing 25% of their length, and then make a heading cut on the leader at a point about 12" to 15" above the top branch you were able to use. Thin out all of those branches you cannot use, either because they are in the wrong place, are broken, or the angle of the crotch is too narrow.

Cultivate and Fertilize

The faster your tree grows, the wider the angles of the new branches will be. So in order to encourage fast growth, take up the grass and cultivate a three foot area around the tree. **Fertilize** it by incorporating a good, partially decayed organic material at planting time or two weeks after you plant with a good tree or shrub fertilizer (read label directions for amount to apply). Place the fertilizer in a loose ring around the tree but don't put any next to the trunk as it could burn the tender bark at the ground line, causing significant and usually fatal injury. A **mulch** of wood bark, wood chips, or grass clippings will also be of great help in maintaining soil moisture, suppressing weeds, and adding organic matter to the soil.

Summer of Year One

Pay close attention to the new shoots as they begin to grow. When any except the top three become 2" long, snap a **spring-loaded clothespin** on the leader just above the new shoot. The clothespin should touch the shoot in order to force it to grow straight out from the

leader instead of turning upward. Remember our little talk about how the sun causes the branch to grow upward? The clothespin **shades the branch** thus preventing injury from the sun, and also **physically holds the branch flat.** This produces a nice wide angle insuring a strong limb. Remove the clothespin when the branch becomes longer than the clothespin and begins to turn toward the sun.

After you remove the pin, you can prop the branch at a 45 degree angle with a round toothpick pointed on both ends [or use a short (6") spreader available commercially, see Appendix]. The toothpick can be left in until the fall. It is good to look the tree over once every week and use the clothespins or toothpicks on new shoots which need spreading.

When the top three new shoots are about 12" long, **cut off two of them.** Leave the top shoot as the leader. Look at the branches you headed this spring. There are three new shoots at the ends of these also; handle them just like the leader – remove all but one.

During the rest of the summer, remove the shoots (suckers) which **grow straight up on top** of the side shoots you chose this spring. They will be too vigorous and will quickly out-grow your other limbs. Make heading cuts on these vertical suckers leaving short stubs with one or two buds.

This is all you have to do during the first season.

Spring of Year Two

Look at all of those new side branches you have to choose from! If you don't have quite a few to choose from, you will need to follow last season's directions again this year ... be sure to make the heading cut on the leader.

This year you want to choose as many **permanent scaffold branches** as possible. **Scaffold branches** are the limbs that will be the main framework of your tree. These are branches you will have to live with for a long time so choose nice, wide crotches and limbs that help balance your tree.

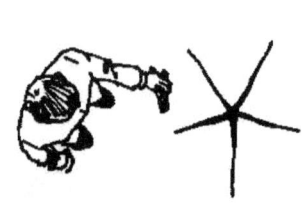 

Star Growth

An apple tree forms buds and therefore branches in a star fashion. If you stand close and look down on the tree from the top you can observe this. Balance is obtained by selecting scaffold branches to maintain the natural star shape. I am not saying that you must choose 5 scaffolds from each year's growth – that would be too many – but rather that as you choose scaffolds over the next 3 to 5 years, you attempt to maintain this star balance.

In the first 3 to 5 years you will need to choose 10 to 12 scaffold branches. Do not head the branches which are growing strongly.

You will, however, have to head back any that tend to be weak. Cut off about 25% of each of these weaker shoots. Always make a dormant-time heading cut on the leader at a point 15" to 18" above the top scaffold. Then remove any branches you do not need. For instance, branches that are too close together or are directly over one another and not at least 12 inches apart. Scaffold branches that are not directly over one another can be as close as 6 inches apart on the leader. Sometimes all of the limbs grow on one side of the tree. If this happens, choose one good limb for a scaffold branch and remove the rest. Then head the leader about 15" above that scaffold. Next year you should be able to choose branches which balance the tree.

Do not remove the short, weak growing shoots which grow on the leader in between the scaffold branches. These will set fruit buds and fruit. They will not interfere with your framework branches. In fact, the extra shade will keep the scaffold branches from becoming more vertical, and the leaves on them will feed the leader, giving you a stronger tree.

Summer of Year Two

This summer, handle the new part of the tree (top) in the same manner as you did the newly planted tree last year. Spread new shoots with clothespins and then toothpicks; remove the narrow angles on the leader and scaffolds when they are 12" long etc.

This year you'll also install **limb spreaders,** and as the limbs on your tree are longer now, you will need longer spreaders than the toothpicks you used to spread last year's growth. We'll use longer limb spreaders to keep the older framework 90° branches at **45 and 55-degree angles.** The 45-degree angle (more horizontal position) is for the more vigorous branches while the 55-degree angle is for the others. The goal is to spread the most flexible portion of the branch in order to keep it at an angle vertical enough to encourage continued shoot extension and yet horizontal enough to allow fruit buds to form on the two-year and older portions of the branch.

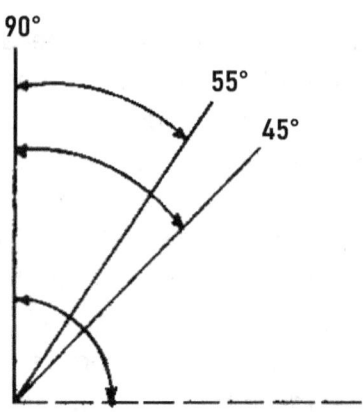

Bending the Twig

Here is a technique that will help you obtain the right angle of the branch, especially when you spread older and stiffer wood. Place the heel of one hand under the branch where you want it to bend and exert pressure on it by pushing. Then with the other hand, pull the branch down over your palm. Do this two or three times. The pressure will crush the phloem tissue on the underside of the branch, weakening it at that point. Now take your pushing hand away and pull down on the branch. Notice that it bends at the weakened spot. The injury to the phloem tissue, by the way, is very temporary. By doing this you take the stress off the crotch area. Without this technique, spreading of the limbs could cause the branch to break at the point of connection with the leader.

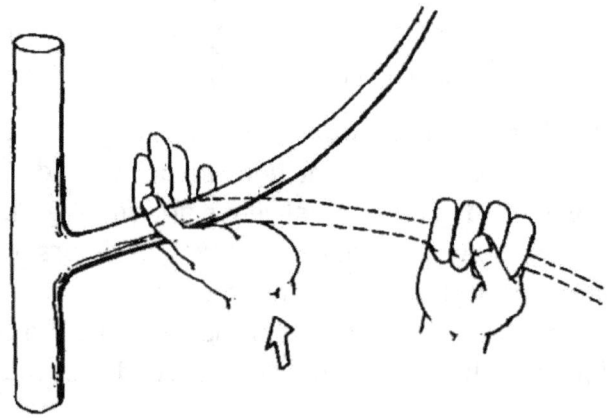

Now stick the end of your *limb spreader* into the wood of the branch just beyond the bend you just made. Push the other end into the leader of the tree at a point which will give you the proper angle for the vigor of the branch.

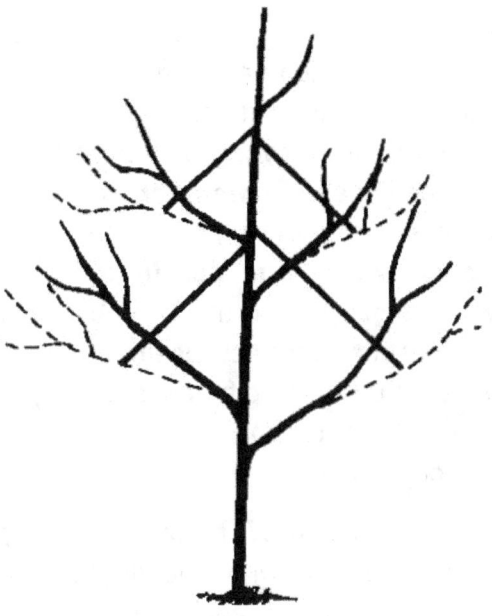

Physical spreading of limbs is effective through about the 5th year. By then the tree should be fruitful enough to keep the branches horizontal. Also after 5 years, the uppermost side branches on the leader are too high to spread easily. However, between the weight of the fruit, summer pruning, and another technique I will describe later, you will be able to control the top of the tree without the need for spreading.

As you may have already guessed, you will have to make longer spreaders each year; these can be purchased commercially (see Appendix), or homemade. Here is one way to make long sturdy spreaders for use on the larger branches in years 3, 4 and 5. Cut some sticks 3/4" by 3/4" and as long as you'll need to spread effectively (i.e., 15", 18", 24", and 36"). Drive a 4-inch long finishing nail into each end leaving about 2" of the nail showing. Cut off the head of the nail with bolt cutters or a hack saw. Be sure to cut on enough of an angle to create a sharp point.

You can also pull limbs into more horizontal positions by tying them down with twine to a stake driven into the ground. This is a good technique where it does not interfere with mowing or other yard activities. **Remember to remove the twine from the branch within one month to prevent girdling.** If the branch does not stay in the new position, re-tie the twine in a different spot on the limb to hold it in the correct position.

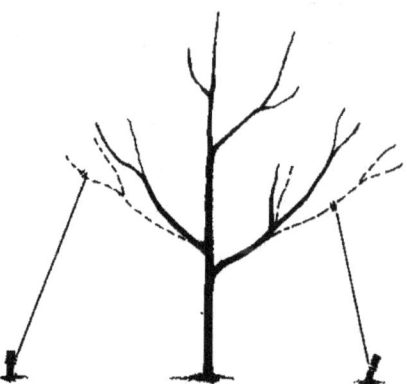

Now let's get back to the second growing year. During the summer, remove with a heading cut the upright suckers growing on the framework branches, leaving a stub with 2 or 3 buds. Also, remove with a thinning cut any growth below the bottom scaffold and any growth from the roots at the base of the tree. Be sure to remove the narrow-angled branches on the leader and any side branches on which you made heading cuts this spring. If there is a branch that is out-growing the others, this is the time to slow it down with a heading cut to keep it in balance with the other limbs.

The Christmas Tree

Our goal is to train the tree to be shaped like a Christmas tree. The lower scaffolds should be longer than those above, etc. ... right on up the tree. If upper branches become longer than the lower ones, the shade will weaken the lower branches to a point where they will have to be removed or

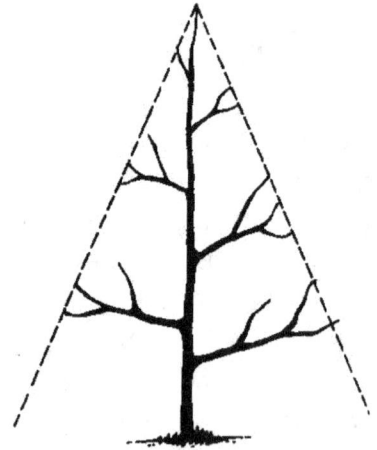

will become unfruitful. Christmas trees have only one stem (leader); all of the other branches are horizontal. This is our goal with the apple tree. That is why we use spreaders and why we remove the upright suckers on the scaffolds and the narrow-angled branches on the leader.

"Always make a dormant time heading cut on the leader at a point 15" to 18" above the top scaffold."

Years Three and Four

During the next two years, continue to prune the tree as in the first two years; last year's wood like the first year, older wood like the second year. Head the leader 12 inches above the top scaffold branch; head back weaker growing branches; remove broken, rubbing, and crowded limbs. Also remove upright shoots growing on the side branches. When upright shoots are removed in the spring use a thinning cut; when removed in the summer use a heading cut. Continue to use spreaders to hold the limbs at 45 and 55-degree angles from the trunk. Allow fruit to grow on the two year and older wood. **Remove all the fruit that sets on last year's wood and on the top 1/3 of the leader of the tree.** The weight of the fruit on the leader will pull it over, destroying the Christmas tree shape.

Continue to summer-head the longer branches in the top to maintain the Christmas tree shape and remove excess sucker growth in the summer. Remember to remove the narrow-angled shoots at the tips of the leader and the side branches which were headed in the spring. Don't remove them until they are at least 12 inches long, or they will not produce enough hormone to insure nice wide-angled crotches of the lower branchlets.

As the tree gets older, the top branches will become more dominant. You see, these branches receive the most sunlight and so are stronger. However, we do not want the top to outgrow the bottom, so when a top branch appears overly large in relation to the bottom, remove it with a thinning cut leaving a weaker growing branch to take its place. **Substituting weak branches for strong branches in the top 1/3 of the tree will be an annual task for the life of the tree.** Remember you can also stimulate the bottom branches to grow more strongly by making numerous heading cuts in the dormant period.

Limit Its Height

You've done a good job training your tree these 4 years, and now it is as tall as you want it to grow. I said I would tell you about a neat way to limit the tree height. The year it reaches 10 to 14 feet (or the height you choose), *do not* remove the narrow angled branches formed on the leader from the dormant heading cut. The next spring, *use a thinning cut to remove the more vigorous of these shoots in the top, leaving the weakest upright shoot.* Then head back the weak upright shoot that's left to only 2 buds. Repeat this procedure of removing the strong and cutting back the weak upright each year. The heading cut is necessary each year to insure new growth from which to choose the following year. *Never remove all of the new shoots at the top of the leader.* If you do, the growth of the tree will be concentrated in the top scaffold branches causing them to overgrow those below, and you will lose the Christmas tree shape of your tree.

Forever After...

Maintenance pruning along with control of the top, consists of removing upright growing suckers and broken or damaged branches, thinning out areas that become too thick to allow enough light into the tree, and summer-heading the higher branches in order to keep them from becoming longer than those below. You should also remove the parts of the bottom branches that touch the ground or are too low to mow under by cutting to a more vertical shoot.

Pruning a Neglected Fruit Tree

Now let's look at some situations you may have in an existing older tree that possibly is not shaped like a Christmas tree, but is instead open-centered and spreading. The usual problem is the presence of too many upright growing limbs that make the tree thick and tall. The natural tendency is to cut these upright branches back in the spring to lower the tree. You now know that this will **aggravate the situation rather than solve your problem, because this stimulates excess vigor** and therefore increases the future height.

So what do you do? Start to thin out some of the upright branches in the spring by completely removing them or by cutting them back to a downward growing limb. In July, remove the upright suckers throughout the tree, and then in August, head back those branches in the top which are longer than the bottom branches and are taller than you want your tree. Remember, pruning in August is a **dwarfing** process. It does not stimulate the excessive vegetative growth that is caused by dormant and early spring cutting.

If you have a crop of apples. head the shoots back to within 5 leaves of the fruit even though this may not shorten the limb as much as you desire.

Repeat this procedure next year and in future years until the tree is back under control. In succeeding years thin out crowding branches and make heading cuts on weaker growing wood. in the spring, remove suckers in July, and control over-vigorous and excessive upright growth with heading cuts in August. Fruit spurs and the fruit need at least 50% full sunlight to develop normally, so keep your trees open. Thin off excess fruit before three weeks after bloom. The fruit you leave on the tree should be at least 5 inches apart on the limbs.

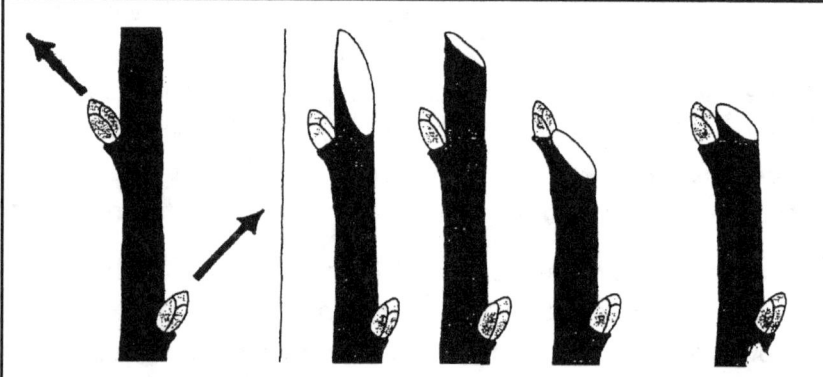

To prune properly, **first select a bud pointing in the direction you wish new growth to go in.** Using clean, sharp pruning shears, cut just above the bud on a slanting line parallel to the bud's direction of growth.

The three pruning cuts on the left are incorrect; the one on the right is made properly. The cut at far left slants too steeply, exposing too much vulnerable heartwood. The next cut is too far from the bud; the stub may not heal. The third cut comes too close to the bud and may cause it to dry out.

The ideal cut, right, starts slightly above the tip of the bud and slants down at a 45° angle, ending level with the base of the bud.

Other Fruit Trees

Pear

Follow the same general procedure as with apples. Pear trees have an upright growth and it will be difficult to find wide angle crotches. This is not as important as it is with apples, however, because pear scaffolds are not prone to splitting. Keep center of tree reasonably open, but resist the temptation to prune the tree top too heavily. New growth caused by excessive pruning is more susceptible to fire blight, which can kill entire branches and trees

At planting, head pear trees at about 24 inches high. If the top is branched, keep three or four branches as scaffolds. Select these scaffolds early in the first summer and carefully spread them. Do little or no pruning except to lightly head and spread the scaffolds annually until the tree starts to bear.

As trees age, shorten or remove upper limbs so they don't shade the lower limbs. Thin out the branches of mature trees, and do the heaviest pruning in the top of the tree. Remove long shoots in the center and top, but leave some short shoots and most spurs. Remove horizontal branches in the top so they won't produce suckers. Invigorate slow-growing spur systems by cutting them back to about half their length, or remove them and replace them with new shoots.

Sweet Cherry

Sweet cherry trees require less pruning than any other fruit tree and very little is done on them the first several years after training. The heading-back of vigorous non-bearing shoots (after harvest) may be desirable to induce more branching, but may result in narrow angled crotches. Dormant heading will result in wider crotch angles.

At planting, head nursery trees at the height you want for scaffold branches. Train sweet cherry trees to the open center system with three to five scaffold branches. Young sweet cherry trees often grow vertical limbs 6 to 8 feet without branching. You must head them to induce lateral branch formation.

Prune in summer to reduce re-growth of vigorous trees. If a young tree is growing very rapidly, cut off a foot or more of new growth after about 3 feet of growth has been made in the summer. This will cause branching. You can hasten production by tying down or weighting limbs to horizontal.

To promote branching on trees not pruned in summer, head every shoot in winter to about 2 feet long. After 5 or 6 years, stop heading, and instead focus on thinning-out crowded branches.

Bacterial canker, a common disease of cherry trees, frequently causes gumming and dead areas or "cankers" on limbs. If it infects the crown or trunk, it can kill the tree. If a gummy, dead area encircles most of a limb, you must cut off the limb.

Mature trees require little pruning except as needed to reduce tree height. If birds are eating a lot of the fruit, you may want to net the tree.

Sour Cherry and European Plum

Sour cherry and European plums require less pruning than apple or pear trees, especially after the main framework of the tree is established. Use the same general methods as for apple. Limit pruning to an annual thinning after the fourth year's growth.

Sour cherry wood is quite brittle, so give special attention to developing wide-angled crotches in young trees. Either select wide-angled shoots to form limbs, or spread shoots to widen the angles. Three main scaffold limbs are enough for a sour cherry tree. The modified central-leader system helps form wide-angled scaffold limbs without having to spread them.

In the first and second summers, remove excess shoots so that all new growth is on the permanent scaffold limbs. In mature trees, only occasional thinning out of excess branches is needed to keep a good balance of light and fruitfulness throughout the tree.

Peach and Japanese Plums

Peach and Japanese plums are pruned by the open center method. With this system, the leader is not allowed to develop. Choose three scaffolds about 18-24 inches above ground, spaced closely together; each should radiate out from the tree in a different direction. The leader should be cut off just above the top scaffold. Select shoots that have the widest angles where they attach to the trunk and that are not all at the same height. Peach limbs with poor crotches are prone to splitting. If branches are large and uniform, leave them about 12 inches long. If they are slender or uneven, cut back to stubs with one or two buds.

The following year, choose shoots that develop from these buds as the main scaffolds. They should be kept at approximately the same length. The mature tree will resemble an upside down umbrella.

Remove scaffold limbs that may compete with the three or four originally selected. Do this in the spring of the second year and again in the third year if necessary. Head the scaffold limbs in the first and second dormant seasons to cause branching until there are 6 to 8 secondary scaffold branches and 12 to 16 tertiary branches.

Every year, prune enough to stimulate new shoot growth for the following year's crop. Peach trees branch readily, so they will have too many weak shoots unless you prune them properly. Thin out shoots, leaving those of moderate vigor. Remove all weak or very strong shoots.

Prune hardest in the top and near the ends of the major limbs. Cut top limbs back to side shoots to stiffen them and reduce tree height. Peach trees crop more consistently and have larger fruits if they're pruned heavily. Commonly, up to 50 percent of the previous season's growth is removed each year.

Peach trees bear fruit only on 1-year-old shoots.

The large size fruit and the brittleness of the limbs on the Japanese plums require the pruning back of fruiting branches to prevent limb breakage.

Apricot

Young apricot trees usually develop many branches in the nursery. Select several of them to be scaffold branches at planting time. Cut these branches back a few inches and remove other branches. One year after planting, cut back long shoots to induce branching. Train the tree as you would for peaches.

Pruning bearing apricot trees is mostly a process of thinning out excess wood and heading long shoots. After a side shoot has produced for 3 or 4 years, remove it and let a new shoot grow in its place.

Persimmon

There are two types of persimmon trees: American and Asian. The Asian persimmon tree is smaller when mature than the American and needs less maintenance pruning to contain its height. Train trees to three to five main scaffold branches.

Fig

Fig trees can be grown with multiple trunks or with single-trunk. If you live in a region with severe freezing weather, grow multiple trunks so that you can thin-out trunks that are damaged or killed ing. In warmer regions, a single-trunk form with three to five scaffold branches is suitable. Be sure to prune the top for good light penetration into the canopy. Figs produce fruit on the current season's shoots, so heading branches to stimulate shoot growth is helpful.

Basic terms

Branch collar—The raised tissue at the base of every branch. It contains specialized cells that seal off pruning wounds from wood rot fungi.

Crotch angle—The angle formed between the trunk and a limb. The strongest crotch angles are between 45 and 60 degrees.

Crown—The base of the trunk where the tree meets the soil.

Heading (or head cut)—A pruning cut that removes only part of a branch.

Lateral branch—A side shoot off of another branch, usually at a more horizontal angle.

Leader—The main stem of a central-leader trained fruit tree.

Root sprout—A one-year-old shoot that grows from the root. These should always be removed as soon as possible.

Scaffold limb—A large limb that forms a tree's framework.

Sucker or Water sprout—A one-year-old shoot that grows within the tree. Typically water sprouts are unproductive and should be removed, either in summer or during the dormant pruning season. This is the one case where leaving a stub of several buds may be useful to change the sucker into productive fruiting wood.

Shoot—The length of branch growth in one season. The bud scale scars (ring of small ridges) on a branch mark the start of a season's growth.

Spur—A short specialized shoot that produces fruit.

Stub—A short portion of a branch left after a pruning cut. In general, avoid leaving stubs when pruning.

Terminal—The end of any shoot.

Thinning cut—A pruning cut that removes an entire branch from its point of origin.

Vertical branch—A branch that grows upright.

Appendix. Training Supplies

A full-range of training supplies, including limb spreaders made of wood, plastic, and metal, is available from **Orchard Innovations**. (*www.orchardinnovations.com*). This online store is operated by the author, with the goal of providing innovative supplies from around the world to small and medium-sized fruit-growers.